STUDIO COMPANION SERIES

PRESENTATION BASICS

BOOK FOUR

STUDIO COMPANION SERIES

||||||||||||||||||||||||||||||||||||||||||||||||||||||||||||||||||||||||||||||||||||

DESIGN BASICS/BOOK ONE

DRAFTING BASICS/BOOK TWO

3D DESIGN BASICS/BOOK THREE

PRESENTATION BASICS/BOOK FOUR

||||||||||||||||||||||||||||||||||||||||||||||||||||||||||||||||||||||||||||||||||||

STUDIO COMPANION SERIES

PRESENTATION BASICS

BOOK FOUR

DONNA LYNNE FULLMER

IIDA, IDEC

KANSAS STATE UNIVERSITY
DEPARTMENT OF INTERIOR ARCHITECTURE
AND PRODUCT DESIGN

FAIRCHILD BOOKS
NEW YORK

Fairchild Books
An imprint of Bloomsbury Publishing Inc

1385 Broadway
New York
NY 10018
USA

50 Bedford Square
London
WC1B 3DP
UK

www.fairchildbooks.com

First published 2014

Library of Congress Cataloging-in-Publication Data
A catalog record for this book is available from the Library of Congress
2013950347
ISBN: PB: 978-1-60901-101-7

Typeset by Precision Graphics
Cover Design by Carly Grafstein
Printed and bound in the United States of America

CONTENTS

vii   PREFACE

ix   ACKNOWLEDGMENTS

ONE – PRESENTATION OVERVIEW

2   OBJECTIVES

3   INTRODUCTION

4   WHO WILL BE AT THE PRESENTATION?

7   WHAT WILL BE PRESENTED?

8   WHERE WILL THE PRESENTATION BE HELD?

9   WHEN WILL THE PRESENTATION BE HELD?

10   TIPS

11   WHY WILL THE PRESENTATION HAPPEN?

12   HOW TO GIVE A PRESENTATION

13   SUMMARY

TWO – VISUAL PRESENTATION SKILLS

14   OBJECTIVES

15   INTRODUCTION

17   DRAWING SELECTION

    18   Plans

    19   Elevations

    20   Sections

    21   Oblique and Axonometric Drawings

    21   One- and Two-Point Perspectives

23   GRAPHIC SYMBOLS

    23   North Arrows

    24   Scales

    25   Elevation Symbols

    26   Section-Cut Symbols

27   TITLES, TEXT, AND LABELS

    27   Project Titles

    28   Drawing Titles

    29   General Text

    30   Labels

    31   Legends and Keys

33 BEGINNING A PRESENTATION

  33 Presentation Layouts

  34 Determining What Is Needed

  35 Cartoon or Mock Presentations

  37 Formatting and Alignment

  38 Grids

  40 Projects with Multiple Sheets

41 SUMMARY

THREE – VERBAL PRESENTATION SKILLS

42 OBJECTIVES

43 INTRODUCTION

45 PREPARATION FOR THE PRESENTATION

  46 Who

  47 What

  47 Where

  48 When

  49 Why

  50 How

52 EXERCISE

55 SUMMARY

FOUR – BUSINESS ETIQUETTE

56 OBJECTIVES

57 INTRODUCTION

58 PRESENTATIONS AND MEETINGS

62 TIPS

63 INDUSTRY AND NETWORKING EVENTS

64 TIPS

65 PHONE AND EMAIL

68 TIPS

69 DINING

73 OTHER ETIQUETTE RULES

75 EXERCISE

77 SUMMARY

FIVE – BODY LANGUAGE

78 OBJECTIVES

79 INTRODUCTION

81 READING FACES

  83 Gestures

85 READING BODIES

  87 Arms

  88 Gestures

90 SUMMARY

91 APPENDIX A: PRESENTATION CHECKLIST

97 APPENDIX B: PRESENTATION BOARD SAMPLES

101 INDEX

PREFACE

|||||||||||||||||||||||||||||||||||||||||||||||||||||||||||||||||||||||||||||||||||||||||||||||||||||||||||||||||||||||||||||||||||||||||||||||||||||||||||||

The overall idea for this series came from the love of teaching the freshman design studio. What I have seen, time and time again, is a lack of basic design skills due to the influx of technology. While I believe in being a well-versed designer, I feel the computer is just another tool in the arsenal of what a student, and a professional, can bring to the table when it comes to designing. To this end, I feel hand skills, and the teaching of hand skills, has become a lost art.

I tell students that beginning the study of architecture and design is like starting kindergarten again, because we ask them to learn to write and draw in a new way. The books in the Studio Companion Series acknowledge that and act as an introduction to a skill through interactive lessons for each topic. I have seen firsthand how students increase their skills more rapidly by doing rather than just seeing. In addition, like it or not, this generation wants things faster and easily digestible. I feel this format, with a lot of images, and text that is direct and simple to read, will play to this audience of future designers.

The Studio Companion Series includes four books that address all the skill sets and topics discussed in beginning the study of architecture and design. Each book is compact, highly portable, and addresses each topic in a clear-cut and graphic manner. Each has been developed for today's students, who want things "down and dirty" and presented in an interactive way with simple examples on the topics. The series includes: *Design Basics, Drafting Basics, 3D Design Basics*, and *Presentation Basics*.

BOOK FOUR: PRESENTATION BASICS

Presentation Basics breaks down the two subtle, yet critical, aspects of a presentation: visual and verbal skills. Students will learn that a good presentation is not just about solid design but it is also about the ablility to graphically represent it well. Beyond the visual skills, students will learn that a strong verbal presentation is required to sell their ideas. All of these factors are addressed, along with an essential look at business etiquette and body language, stressing the impact they can have on a presentation.

ACKNOWLEDGMENTS

The Studio Companion Series is the result of working with students all over the country and the thrill I get watching the "light bulbs go on" as they learn. There is nothing like seeing a student properly use a scale for the first time—being a part of this type of learning is an addiction. To all my students, thank you for giving me that charge and making me proud!

To my high school English teacher and to the men and women I work alongside every day, thank you for showing me how to listen to students and respond respectfully while maintaining the authority in the classroom.

To Olga Kontzias and Joseph Miranda, thank you for your constant support and understanding through the entire Studio Companion Series. They would not exist without you. To Olga, especially, we have come from an informal chat three years ago to a published series of four books. Thank you for your personal faith in the project!

Finally, everyone writes and says this, but I owe my career to my supportive and loving family, who have taught me things you could never find in a textbook.

STUDIO COMPANION SERIES

PRESENTATION BASICS

BOOK FOUR

ONE

PRESENTATION OVERVIEW

OBJECTIVES

You will be able to identify and understand:

- The basics of design presentations
- The who, what, when, where, why, and how of preparing to give a presentation

THE FIRST YEAR OF DESIGN SCHOOL IS ABOUT LEARNING HOW TO DRAW YOUR IDEAS; BUT EQUALLY IMPORTANT IS THE ABILITY TO COMMUNICATE THOSE IDEAS BOTH VISUALLY AND VERBALLY. IN THIS CHAPTER, THE VISUAL ASPECT OF PRESENTATIONS WILL BE ADDRESSED. HOWEVER, THE WAY YOU DRAW AND LAY OUT YOUR VISUAL PRESENTATION HAS A DIRECT CONNECTION TO HOW YOU WILL PRESENT IT VERBALLY. THE OLD ADAGE ABOUT KNOWING THE WHO, WHAT, WHERE, WHEN, WHY, AND HOW HIGHLIGHTS IMPORTANT ASPECTS TO CONSIDER WHEN PREPARING TO GIVE A PRESENTATION.

WHO WILL BE AT THE PRESENTATION?

First, think about *to whom* you will be presenting. Typically, your audience will fall into two major categories: those who understand design vocabulary—your peers, faculty members, and the architectural and design community; and those who do not—the general public and your clients.

Other things to take into consideration are, will you be the one presenting the project, and if so, will you be alone or with a team? What role, if any, do the other team members play? Will your presentation be taken back to a client's office so they can show it to others, or will be it pinned up somewhere for feedback without a formal verbal presentation?

© iStockphoto.com/izusek

Knowing this information will make it easier to move forward with the presentation and delegate to each team member. Knowing if the presentation needs to stand on its own will help you determine whether additional drawings or text are needed to support your design without the benefit of you being there to present it.

© iStockphoto.com/CEFutcher

Finally, how many people will be at the presentation, and what form will the presentation take? Will there be a table with a panel of jurors, a room of a dozen other students, a large room with a dozen other students' work alongside yours being judged by the public and the design community?

Knowing the number of people and preferred presentation format will allow you to prepare an effective presentation. If the presentation will be done electronically, always save the file in a common format such as a PDF to ensure that all the images and text are embedded. Check this by emailing it to yourself and opening it on another computer. If possible, bring your own computer to use at the presentation. Finally, always bring a printed copy of your electronic presentation and enough copies for the intended audience.

All of these issues need to be answered so that you know how to put your presentation together, and each of these scenarios can happen during your first year of study.

WHAT WILL BE PRESENTED?

In your first year of study, *what* will be presented may be dictated to you, or there may be some freedom for you to decide. Obviously, this is the major aspect of this chapter, but in this category you should look at all the types of items that can be presented and the methods by which they can be delivered. Will you present a project sheet or board, or a series of them; a model that may or may not have removable parts; an electronic presentation where you need a computer and a projector; samples of materials being used for the design; or any other visual aids? The actual creation of the presentation is a very detailed process, and you may use many of these methods to communicate your design intent.

© iStockphoto.com/Michal_edo

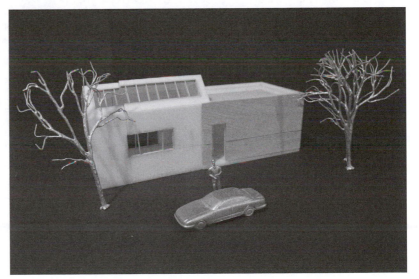

WHERE WILL THE PRESENTATION BE HELD?

This may seem like a trivial aspect to consider when you are creating your presentation, but location is everything. I attended a presentation that was done outside, where several students lost portions of their projects due to the wind, and several projects got faded from the sun. This is obviously an extreme example, but it illustrates the point very well.

The location of your presentation can dictate what you will present. Also for consideration is what will the location offer you in terms of supplies? Will the room or space have thumbtacks to use to hang boards, or will there be an easel or ledge to lean the boards against? One professor became obsessed with the placement of the pins students were using when they pinned their boards up. The pins had to be not just in order and level, but placed in the exact same spot on every board.

For some in your audience, attending an architectural presentation is like watching a foreign film. You do not want to lose their attention by distracting them with a crooked board or seating them too far away to see the subtitles. The bottom line is you want to have a positive presentation, which may include the use of a backup plan. Make sure you have thought of every scenario that can, and will, happen at your presentation.

© iStockphoto.com/quavondo

WHEN WILL THE PRESENTATION BE HELD?

For presentations, this comes down to time management. *When* you have to present a project is a crucial thing to understand before you begin.

Ask yourself several questions:

- Are you producing all the work, and have you allocated enough time to get the project done?

- If you are working on a team, have you all agreed on who is doing what and when it needs to be complete?

- Do you have access to any printers and plotters you need to use?

- Do you have all the supplies you need to create the presentation, or do you need to order them from somewhere or pick them up at a store before you begin?

Once you have determined all of this you can begin your presentation. Start by making a list of things to do and create a master calendar with all the crucial due dates. Share this calendar with all of the team members and your professor, while in school. This will help everyone stay on track and hold them accountable for their parts of the presentation.

© iStockphoto.com/Kate_sept2004

If any part of the presentation is being done electronically with software like AutoCAD or Revit, make sure you establish a common file storage space and a naming system for the files or layers. Set these aspects up ahead of time so there is no confusion. Again, while in school, this may be established already for you.

© iStockphoto.com/mediaphotos

TIPS:

- As you start in your first year of study, keep a notebook with the title of each item you have to work on at the top. Then write the time you start and stop working on it. At the end of the project you can add the hours up to see how long it took you to complete each item, which will help you on the next project to budget your time better.

- Create a calendar with crucial dates and make it a common calendar, if it is a team project. Adjust that calendar as a team as the project progresses.

WHY WILL THE PRESENTATION HAPPEN?

There are several reasons *why* you need to present your project. First, it could be a simple "pin-up" critique presentation, which means a less formal presentation that may just be for your class. Often, the purpose of these is to check the status of everyone's project. They can be impromptu or scheduled.

Second, it can be a final presentation at the end of the year where you need to dress in a professional manner to present to a jury of design professionals. This is more formal and scheduled to provide you with more in-depth feedback.

Lastly, it could be a public exhibit outside of school where you will be interacting with, as well as presenting to, alumni and the design community. This type of presentation can be either formal or informal depending on the situation, but in either case several students could be presenting simultaneously to small groups of people or individuals.

In college, your professors should be able to identify the "why" aspect of the presentations, which may not be obvious to you at the time, but ultimately will lead up to your grade in the course. In the industry, presentations are given at the various stages of the design process. A more comprehensive list of the design process and the presentation types given at each phase can be found in Chapter Three of *Design Basics,* book one in the Studio Companion Series.

HOW TO GIVE A PRESENTATION

IIIIIIIIIIIIIIIIIIIIIIIIIIIIIIIIIIIIIIIIIIIIIIIIIIIIIIIIIIIIIIIIIIIIIIIIIIIIIIIIIIIIIIIIIIIIIIIIIIIIIIIIIIIIIIIIIIIIIIII

This is a loaded question with many answers that will be explored in the rest of this book. Suffice to say, you will always present visually and verbally. The visual aspect requires you to look at the who, what, where, when, and why to get to the *how* portion of preparing for a presentation. The following chapters will outline this through these major categories:

- How to select the correct drawings that should be presented
- How to strengthen the drawings through the use of graphic symbols
- How to strengthen the project through the use of titles, text and labels
- How to layout a successful presentation
- How to verbally sell your design while keeping your body language in mind

SUMMARY

||||||||||||||||||||||||||||||||||||||||||||||||||||||||||||||||||||||||||||||||||||||||||||||||||||||||||||||||||||||||||||||||||||

Gaining an understanding of presentation skills is very important to the degree of success you will have as a designer. It is not only about being able to design but also about being able to sell that design to whomever you are presenting, in any location, and under any condition. Visual and verbal presentation skills are about making every essential aspect of your presentation count.

TWO

VISUAL PRESENTATION SKILLS

OBJECTIVES

You will be able to identify and create:

- A variety of visually successful presentations

- Organized and thoughtfully selected orthographic and paraline drawings

- Well-placed graphic symbols to communicate your design intent

- Text that is appropriate to support your drawings and project

VISUAL PRESENTATION SKILLS ARE VERY IMPORTANT TO THE SUCCESS YOU WILL SEE AS A DESIGNER. YOU HAVE TO SELECT THE DRAWINGS, MODELS, AND OTHER VISUAL AIDS YOU WILL PRESENT TO MAKE SURE THE VIEWER UNDERSTANDS YOUR DESIGN INTENT. THE LAYOUT AND ORDER IN WHICH ITEMS ARE PRESENTED IS CRITICAL, EVEN DOWN TO THE TEXT SIZE USED ON YOUR DRAWINGS AND THROUGHOUT YOUR PRESENTATION.

In general, there are two types of drawings used in design: presentation drawings and technical drawings. Presentation drawings are graphic in content and are not meant to be used to build the project, but instead sell the idea of the design intent. Construction drawings, or technical drawings, are used to build the project and contain other types of information. While both types of drawings use the same basic orthographic and paraline drawings, they obviously have different intents. This chapter will address the major aspects of presentation drawings specifically.

DRAWING SELECTION

You want to communicate your design clearly to the intended audience. The easiest way to do so is to utilize your drawings. Book two in the Studio Companion Series, *Drafting Basics,* looked at all the two-dimensional orthographic drawings you can create of a space, including plans, elevations, and sections. Book three in the series, *3D Design Basics,* looked at all the three-dimensional paraline

drawings you can create to see the space, including axonometrics, obliques, and one- and two-point perspectives. For review, here are some of those drawings of the one-bedroom cabin that have been used throughout the series of books.

You will select from these and other drawings of the one-bedroom cabin to communicate your design.

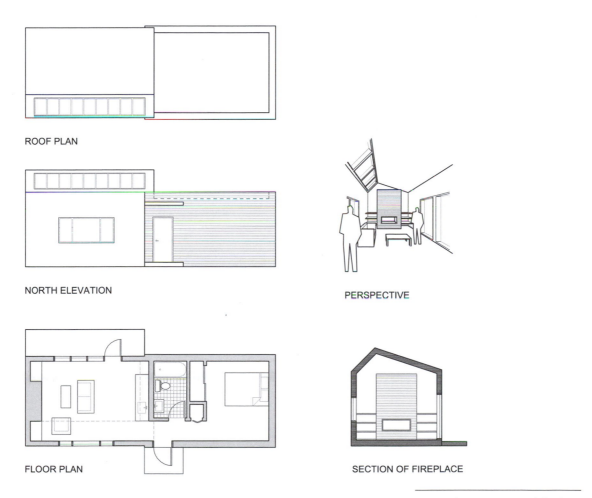

ROOF PLAN

NORTH ELEVATION

PERSPECTIVE

FLOOR PLAN

SECTION OF FIREPLACE

PLANS

An overall floor plan should be used in almost all cases to orient the viewer to the space and to show the relationships among the spaces within a building. It will provide an overall understanding of the length and width of the space.

An enlarged plan, seen on the right, can also be used to give more detailed design information, like a tile pattern on a bathroom floor. The drawing scale can be adjusted for clarity, depending on the drawing use.

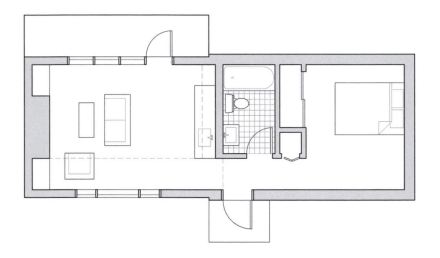
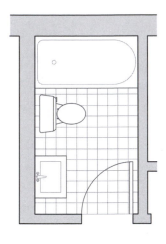

The plan can include many graphic symbols, which will be discussed later in this chapter, to allow for greater understanding and proper referencing among the drawings used throughout the entire presentation.

ELEVATIONS

Elevations can be used whenever you are trying to communicate what is happening with the height of the space or design. If all the walls in a space are finished with one color of paint, as in the bedroom of the cabin—with the exception of window and door placement—you may not need to draw the elevations, because the walls will all be finished the same. The plan and exterior elevations or axonometric drawings will indicate the locations of the windows and doors, so there is no need to be redundant by adding more drawings. However, in the large living space there is a fireplace with built-in shelving on the west wall and a kitchen on the east wall. Elevations would be needed to ensure that the client understands the location and heights of these items.

Through the thoughtful selection of the right combination of drawings, you can communicate the design intent properly.

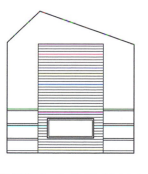
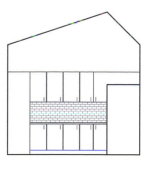

FIREPLACE WALL   KITCHEN WALL

SECTIONS

Sections are used when you want to show the construction or relationships of one space to another. For our cabin the relationships are fairly simple, but they can get very complex in a larger space or taller building. Sections are probably one of the hardest drawings for clients and non–designers to understand. For our one-bedroom cabin a section may be used to show the relationships in heights from room to room, because the floor plan already shows the relationship of the rooms to one another.

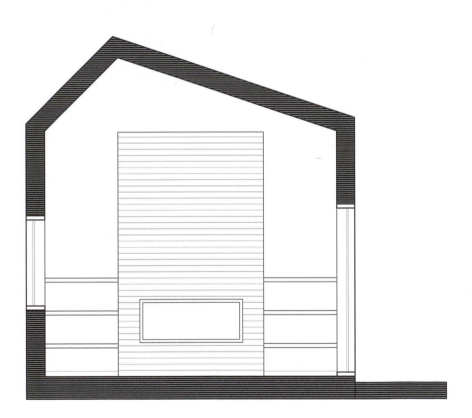

OBLIQUE AND AXONOMETRIC DRAWINGS

These two types of drawings allow for a three-dimensional view of the space as if someone were looking down on it. For presentations, they give a good understanding of the overall form and shape of the space or building, but they do not give a good understanding as it relates to a person using the space.

In some cases these drawings can be simplified and made into diagrams to reinforce the major design forms or zones of the space.

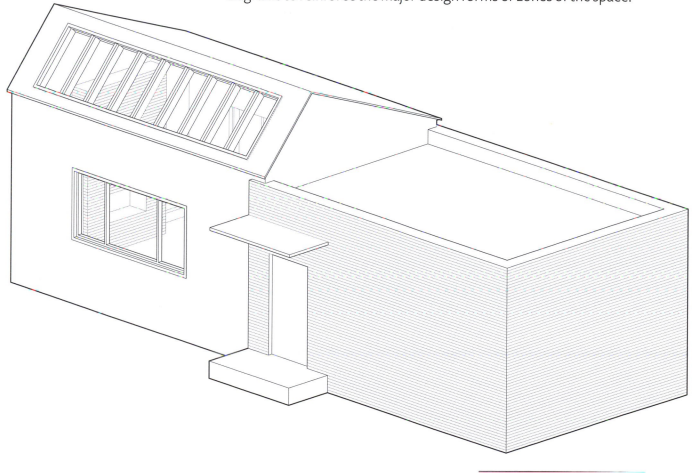

ONE- AND TWO-POINT PERSPECTIVES

One- and two-point perspectives are three-dimensional drawings that take the viewer's vantage point into account to show the human and visual scale of the space. They are the most easily understandable drawings a designer can use to communicate his or her designs. Several drawing views should be used throughout the presentation for clarity. Remember to always include people, and other entourage, in every single drawing to increase the viewer's understanding of the space. This is explained, step-by-step, in the third book in the Studio Companion Series, *3D Design Basics*.

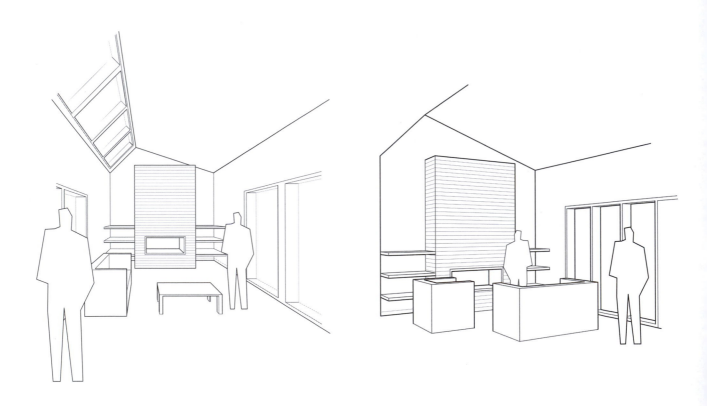

GRAPHIC SYMBOLS

Within any drawing, you will find many different symbols. Although architects, engineers, drafters, and contractors will have their own versions of each of these symbols, they will still function consistently with the standards listed below. In design presentation drawings these symbols tend to have a little more flair than they do in construction drawings, so they can be simplified from what is seen here to suit your own design style or the style of the project.

NORTH ARROWS

A north arrow does exactly what you'd expect: it indicates which direction is north on a plan. This applies to a plan only, even though there can be many different kinds of plans: floor plans, furniture plans, site plans, to name a few. Remember to strive to always have the plans oriented with north pointing up, just like on maps.

Though the north arrow can be found in many different styles and versions, below are some of the most common:

From left to right, here is how to create these types of basic north arrow:

- Draw an arrowhead using your 45-degree triangle and T-square and poché in the triangle, then add below the triangle an "N" indicating north.

- Draw a circle and divide in half. Create the angle legs of the arrow using your 45-degree triangle and poché in the triangle, then add an "N" below that.

- Draw a circle using your circle template and divide into quarters. Draw a heavier line on the side that points north and add the letter "N" to confirm that direction.

NOTE: North arrows are typically placed below one of the lower corners of a plan.

SCALES

A scale can be the actual measured scale that was used to create the drawing, or it can be a more graphic representation of the scale, as shown below.

$$\frac{1}{4}" = 1'\text{-}0"$$

To indicate the scale, simply write it out or draw it graphically by measuring out each of the first divisions of the scale and then doing the same for the total units of the scale itself. In the example above, there are four divisions, with every other one being pochéd for the first four, indicating the scale at $\frac{1}{4}" = 1'\text{-}0"$. Then there is a segment an inch long, which represents four feet, and so on, alternating every four feet.

Scales should be used on every drawing, with the exception of perspective drawings, as they have no final scale, although one might have been started with a true scale to ensure accuracy.

Scales are typically placed below each drawing name and, for a plan, should be located below the opposite side of the north arrow. This can be seen in the section "Titles, Text, and Labels" later in this chapter.

ELEVATION SYMBOLS

Elevation symbols are used to indicate an elevation drawing on a plan ONLY. The symbol indicates on the plan the point of view shown by the elevation, and can include information to help the viewer understand where the drawing is located within the presentation. The arrowhead points in the direction the viewer is looking. In order to know you are pointing in the correct direction, pretend the arrowhead is your feet standing in the floor plan. As a reminder, these symbols can be used in technical drawings, but here they are simple and graphic.

In the example below, the elevation is being referred to as the second elevation seen on the presentation, as indicated by the number two seen beside the arrow.

The image on the left shows examples of the graphic symbols themselves, while the image on the right shows the symbols in context with the plan, followed by the properly labeled elevation itself. Both drawings can stand on their own in a presentation but rely on each other for the viewer's understanding of the project.

   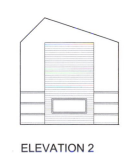

ELEVATION 2

To draw an elevation symbol as seen above, create an arrowhead as you did for the north arrow and put the number or letter of the elevation beside or below it. This can occur within a circle just like the north arrow, or it can be without it.

SECTION-CUT SYMBOLS

A section-cut symbol is used to indicate where a section was cut on the floor plan and the direction in which the drawing is viewed. The title or name of the section drawing should reference the indicator from the plan in a presentation. In the example below, the section is being referred to as the B section seen on the presentation. As with the elevations, the image on the left shows the graphic symbols by themselves, while the image on the right shows the symbol in context with the plan and then the actual section properly labeled. Here again, the drawings can stand on their own, but together they enhance the viewer's understanding of the project.

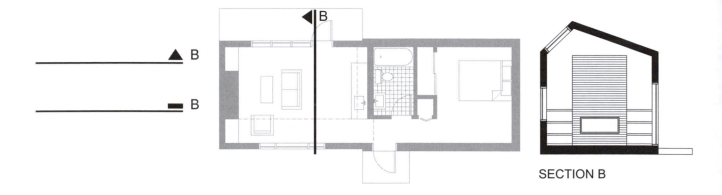

SECTION B

To draw a section-cut symbol as seen above, create a line through the plan where the section was cut and add an arrowhead or heavy line in the direction of the view the drawing was taken. Finally, put the number or letter of the section cut for proper reference.

The section-cut symbol should be placed on the floor plan ONLY as seen above.

TITLES, TEXT, AND LABELS

As we have discussed earlier, project presentations can vary. For the sake of simplicity, there is only one version being used in this chapter to illustrate all the components needed in a presentation. Consult the Appendices for a full variety of options, but keep in mind that project presentations should include the drawings, symbols, and items discussed in this chapter.

PROJECT TITLES

Project titles are typically the largest text on the sheets or boards. A title represents the large, overall idea for the project. For our one-bedroom cabin, the project title could be any of the following: Mountain Retreat, Cabin by the Sea, Smith Summer Home, and the list could go on and on. Details such as the size of the cabin, exact location, design details, etc., are not fully known from the project title.

Place the project title anywhere it makes sense to you as the designer to anchor your presentation. You can add your name or firm name, semester, course, professor name or any other information relevant to the entire project. This will be discussed in more depth later in the chapter.

Mountain Cabin

Student Name

Fall 2013

Professor Name

ENVD 201

Mountain Cabin

Student Name

Fall 2013

Professor Name

ENVD 201

DRAWING TITLES

Unlike the project title, drawing titles are used throughout the presentation, on each and every drawing. They are typically drawn with ¼"-high letters but can be increased or decreased depending on the distance the presentation will be viewed from (although ¼" is usually sufficient).

The drawing titles can be located above or below, and to the left or the right, of the drawings. Whichever you choose, try to be consistent in their location to further assist in the viewer's understanding of your presentation.

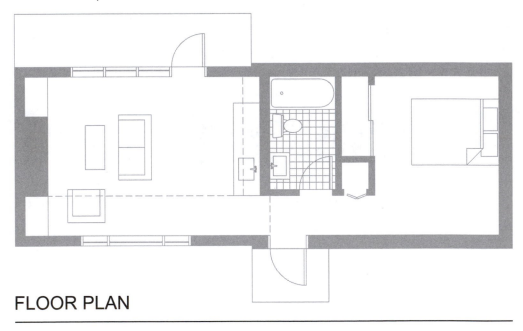

FLOOR PLAN

Scale: 1/8" - 1'-0"

The layout of the boards, and therefore the titles, will be discussed later in this chapter, but there is some flexibility in varying the location of the drawing titles if the layout warrants it.

GENERAL TEXT

There may be a need to add general text to your presentation. This could include a design concept statement, a description of the site or location, or a list of furniture or finishes used on the project. No matter what information it conveys, the text should be consistent, first, within its context, but second, within the project. Larger text will draw attention, so determine if that is necessary in a particular area; the project title, for example, is more important than the types of furniture used in the space.

In the layout portion of this chapter this will become more apparent.

LABELS

In some cases a few labels may be needed to enhance a drawing or indicate specific items. In presentation drawings they should be used sparingly but may be necessary. Remember to consider the size of the text and if a leader, or line, is needed to point out an area. If so, make it proportional to the drawing and other text in that area.

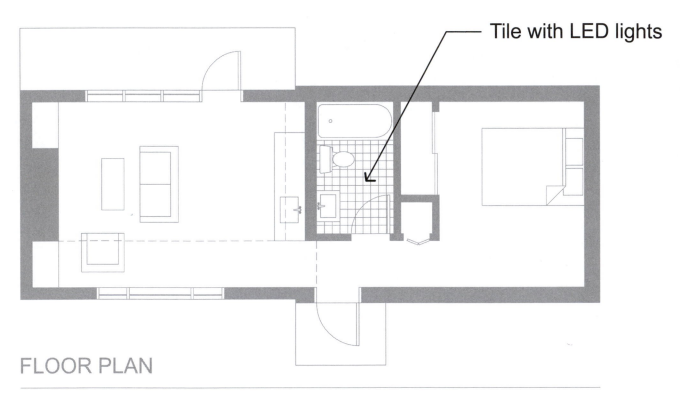

Tile with LED lights

FLOOR PLAN

Scale: 1/8" - 1'-0"

LEGENDS AND KEYS

A legend or key may be needed to clarify a drawing. This is typically done in one of two formats: a list with text in columns, or a graphic symbol with text clarifying that symbol. Both can be used within a presentation, depending on what you want to communicate to the viewer.

On a floor plan, for example, a list may be used to indicate the rooms within a plan, and a key could be used to explain what the letters indicate on the plan.

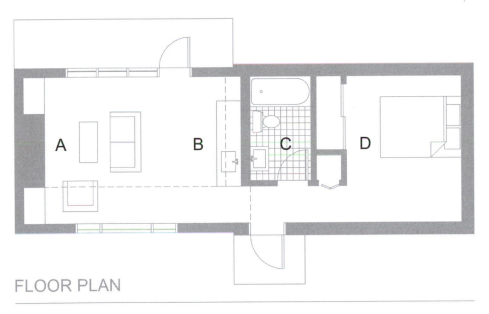

Legend:

A   Living Room
B   Kitchen
C   Bathroom
D   Bedroom

FLOOR PLAN

Scale: 1/8" - 1'-0"

Also, a series of graphic symbols could be used on a floor plan to indicate different floor finishes, and a small legend could be used for that.

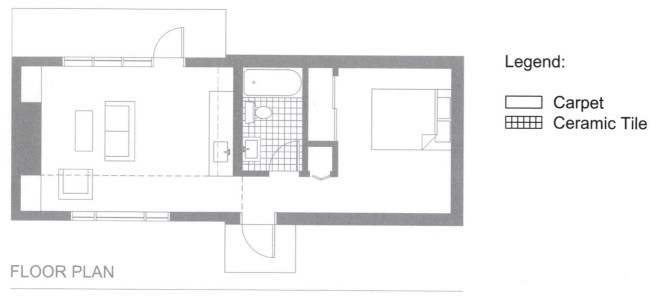

Legend:

▭ Carpet
▦ Ceramic Tile

FLOOR PLAN

Scale: 1/8" - 1'-0"

In either case, legends and keys are used to clarify the drawing and strengthen the design intent. Without them, the drawings would not be fully understood.

BEGINNING
A PRESENTATION

When you first think about your presentation, think about what you want to communicate to your viewers. There are two major approaches to setting up your presentation: The first is "walking" viewers through the project as it might be unveiled to them if they were actually using the space. The second is to drive home a design concept with an overall view of where the project idea came from and how it is laid out in your design. You should go back to this goal every time you make a decision for your presentation layout. Regardless of which approach you choose, select only drawings and items that will assist you with your presentation and ensure full design understanding from the client.

PRESENTATION LAYOUTS

The idea of "walking" a client through a presentation might mean that the first item you show them is a floor plan. Verbally, you would begin by showing them the front door, followed by the path they would take to the kitchen. Later, as your presentation progresses, you could show them how to get to the bedroom from the living area and then to the bathroom. You can point out design features as you go by adding an elevation and an enlarged floor plan of the bathroom, which could indicate wall washers in the hallway and LED-embedded floor tiles that eliminate the need to turn on the overhead lights. This combination of drawings tells the story of how the client will use the space. Without all these drawings that story would not be known.

This is in contrast to how to present the project with the overall design concept in mind. In this scenario you might first present an axonometric of the entire space while discussing the fact that the client's interaction within the building makes the space come alive. The same wall washers and LED tiles could then be presented in step-by-step perspective drawings as you discuss how the client's passing by or entering the space makes these items work.

Both presentations are effective, and the choice depends on not only the designer, but the client as well. Each should be considered and perhaps even attempted before the final presentations are complete.

DETERMINING WHAT IS NEEDED

Most designers will create a simple list of drawings they think they will present. A floor plan will almost always be presented, but where it is located within the presentation could be up for discussion.

The easiest way to start a presentation is to create the list of drawings needed. Appendix A provides a comprehensive list of drawings and other items that may be used in a presentation, which should be the jumping-off point to begin your layout for your design. I suggest making a copy of the list to take notes on for each presentation you will make. Check the items needed and indicate the quantity you might need. As an example, if you have designed a two-story space you will have at least two floor plans (see Appendix A).

CARTOON OR MOCK PRESENTATIONS

Once the list is complete with what you think you will need to present, preparing a cartoon or mock set of the layout will make life simpler as you compile and complete the items needed for your presentation.

Most people begin with a simple template of the overall length and width of the sheet or board they are required to present. This chapter assumes you will be printing out or actually drawing the presentation. Electronic presentations using software like PowerPoint or Prezi are very popular, but this book focuses on physical presentations. However, the basics of strategy and layout can be applied to electronic presentations as well, and in some cases templates and snap guides are built into the programs. It is much more important to know the principles of design presentation layouts then it is to know the software used to create them. As with anything else, software is a tool to get you to a good presentation; understanding the principles is the most important thing.

To begin a mock presentation you will need to know the size and orientation of the boards you are required to use. For this example, we will use

18" × 24" boards, which are seen here in both portrait and landscape orientations.

The size is important, for obvious reasons, but in addition, the orientation could determine if a drawing needs to be spread between two or more sheets of the presentation. If that needs to occur, the drawing, and where it should be cut, should be chosen wisely.

The next step is to determine the overall size and shape of the drawings and other items you will use. Consult the list you have created and make a basic shape, to scale, of each drawing you will require.

The drawings seen below are ghosted with the overall rectangle of the space highlighted to see what size would be used for the mock set.

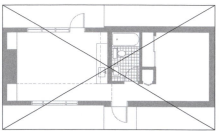 

For text, consult older projects to see how much space other text has taken up and adjust up or down based on the quantity of text for this project.

Create a boundary for every item that will be part of your presentation. This boundary is to real scale. So if the floor plan is 20"- 0" by 36"- 0" at ¼" scale, it is actually 5" × 9" to real scale. This will make it easier to put a variety of scaled drawings and items together on the final presentation.

Now begin to place the drawings and other items onto the overall board or sheet. If you have the luxury of the space to do this at full scale please do so by mounting it on a wall so you can step away and look at the simple lines and spacing of the project.

If you must reduce the scale due to space constraints, do so to every item being used. This means if the final board is going to be 18" × 24" and you need to do the layout at half scale, the layout sheet will be 9" × 12", which means you also need to scale down the basic shapes you measured for each drawing or item by half. This will get easier and easier the more you do it.

Now simply draw each shape onto the board, remembering the goal of the presentation. Some people create the overall shape of each drawing or item out of a separate sheet of paper so they can constantly move them around. If you do this, trace the shapes for each possible "final" layout and set the tracing aside until you come up with the perfect layout.

FORMATTING AND ALIGNMENT

No matter which drawings you select or which presentation format you choose, you want to make sure the overall look of the presentation is clean, aligned, and easy to read. As you lay out each item make sure you have the same distance from the edge of the paper to edge of the drawings—on the sides and at the top and bottom. If a drawing is not the same size as any other, align them to one side. These all do not need to be equal distances, but the spacing on the sides should be consistent as well as the spacing at the top and bottom.

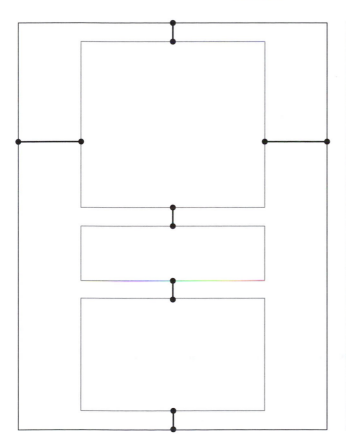

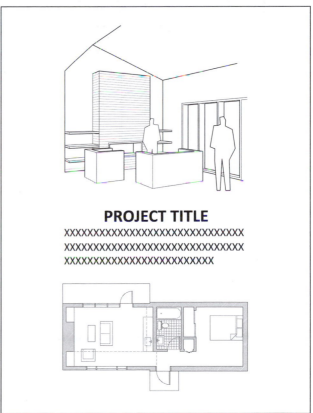

PROJECT TITLE

XXXXXXXXXXXXXXXXXXXXXXXXXXXXXXX
XXXXXXXXXXXXXXXXXXXXXXXXXXXXXXX
XXXXXXXXXXXXXXXXXXXXXXXXXXX

GRIDS

A formal grid can be established that can be used from sheet to sheet. Whatever way the grid is used can vary. You can be very basic and set up a one-by-one grid, which makes it fairly easy to lay out a board. Or you can create a grid that caters more to the dimensions of your project.

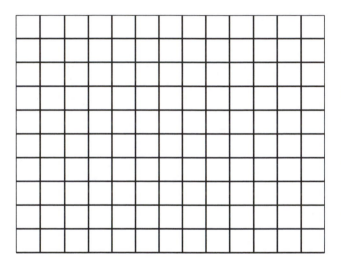

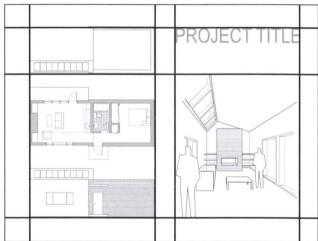

The left drawing is a simple one-by-one grid that gives you the optimal layout options. Individual drawings can take up several areas within the grid the grid while still aligning.

The layout on the right is specific to the drawings used for the presentation.

Do not crowd your sheets. Use a common spacing on all four of
the outer edges and a minimum between drawings to allow each to
breathe, so to speak, and to carry its own weight on the page. Seen
below are good (left) and bad (right) presentation layouts.

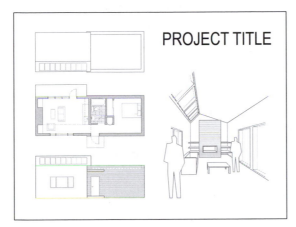

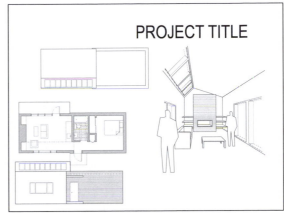

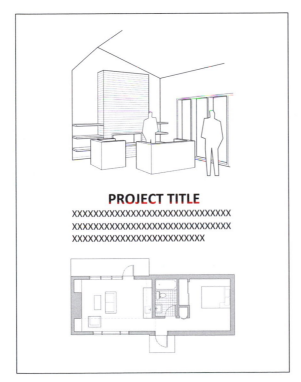

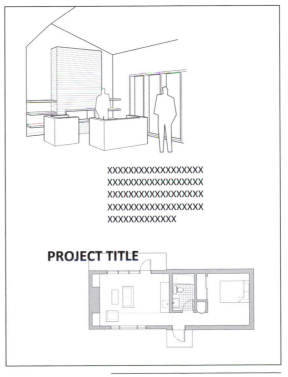

PROJECTS WITH MULTIPLE SHEETS

When spreading a project across multiple sheets, keep in mind how that affects the success of the presentation. Be aware of breaking up drawings and make logical choices that still allow the drawings to read.

Use legends at the bottom or on the back of the boards so you know how to pin them up for the actual presentation. You may have people assisting you, or the client wishes to take the boards back to their office or business, so you want to make sure they are laid out properly. A simple border at the base of each board or a layout guide on the back could be helpful to assist with this.

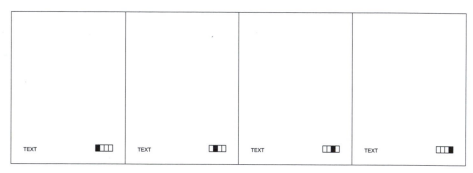

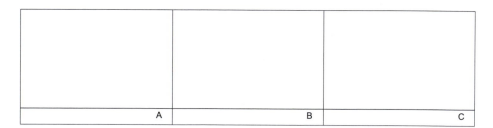

Remember, it is sometimes the simplest things that can ruin all the hard work you have put into a project. Try to keep that possibility to a minimum by controlling what you can.

SUMMARY

|||||||||||||||||||||||||||||||||||||||||||||||||||||||||||||||||||||||||||||||||||||||||||||||||

The visual presentation you create will sell your project as you speak about it. It must graphically demonstrate your design intent in a clear and concise way while enhancing your client's understanding of the project. Make sure the presentation includes everything you want to present and get the client's approval prior to moving on to the next stage of the project. The stages of the project are discussed in detail in *Design Basics,* book one of the Studio Companion Series.

Finally, use your layout to prompt you to discuss key ideas or issues. There is no need to include something you won't discuss. If it is presented it should be discussed.

THREE

VERBAL PRESENTATION SKILLS

OBJECTIVES

You will be able to identify and prepare:

- Organized and thoughtful verbal presentations
- Presentations free of distractions
- Presentations for a variety of audiences

As discussed in Chapter One, giving a presentation is a critical part of your design education. The preparation of the presentation has to be thought of in two major areas: the visual and the verbal. Chapter Two looked into the visual aspect, while this chapter will cover the verbal portion. They should be done in tandem with one another to ensure the best results. When laying out your presentations, you should be thinking of what you are going to say in order to allow the visuals to aid in keeping your verbal presentation on track. This is true if you are presenting physical boards and models or an electronic file.

In addition, remember to consider the who, what, where, when, why, and how as a good way to start preparing for a presentation. The verbal part of the presentation is clearly the "how," but the others are equally important and covered in other portions of this book.

Finally, identifying any weaknesses you may have when it comes to public speaking, and practicing to eliminate them, will result in better design presentations.

PREPARATION FOR THE PRESENTATION

A strong verbal presentation should be clear, concise, and well thought out, and should include the following:

- The successful use of visual aids, which are discussed in this chapter, including design boards, models, samples, an electronic presentation or demonstration

- An introduction of yourself and, if you were on a design team, the rest of the members

- A strong opening statement about the overall design concept, and introducing the problem, if there was one

- Discussion of the key aspects of the design, which should be supported by your visual aid choices

- A thoughtful conclusion to the presentation with a summary of the overall project concept and design intent

- A sincere thank-you to the audience

- An invitation for any comments or questions

In addition, addressing the who, what, where, when, and why, as discussed in Chapter One, will assist in the creation of a successful verbal presentation.

WHO

There are two major aspects in the verbal presentation that relate to the "who" component. First, do the audience members have a design vocabulary, like your fellow students, designers, and teachers, or don't they, like some clients? You should always use your design vocabulary, but you can tailor it to educate the people who are not familiar with it.

In a statement to your fellow design students you could say, "The offices are located along a datum," which is something they will understand without clarification. To a client you could say, "All the office doors open to a common hallway, which is referred to as a 'datum,' an architectural organization method," so they learn the meaning of the term.

Second, you need to determine if you will be presenting alone or as a group. If you are presenting alone, you can proceed with your presentation, making sure you address all the requirements. If you are presenting as a team, you will need to make sure there is a common voice from all the members regarding the design concept and project.

© iStockphoto.com/diane39

WHAT

The choice of the visual aids will greatly affect the verbal presentation. You should lay out the visual aspects to act as cues for the verbal presentation. Beginning with a perspective drawing will make it easier to understand for someone without strong design knowledge while you verbally discuss the big design concept. Conversely, you can present the floor plan or diagram first when explaining your concept to fellow students who have that design vocabulary and understanding of those drawings.

The best verbal presentation supports the visual presentation, and vice versa. The only time this is not true is obviously when the presentation will be viewed without the benefit of you being there to support it. That should change greatly the visual aspect of your presentation.

© iStockphoto.com/Georgijevic

WHERE

Where you will be doing your presentation could have some impact on the verbal presentation.

Depending on the size of the location, a microphone might be needed. Find out as far in advance as possible if this will be the case. If you need one, find out if it will be hand-held or attached to your clothing, so that you can practice. The type of microphone could impact your ability to hold a model or point to areas of your presentation, so getting comfortable with the situation is critical.

Get to the location as early as you have access, so you can set up properly. If the current setup does not work for you, ask if you can rearrange the room. Use the room effectively by making eye contact with the audience. Make them feel engaged. While presenting, make sure everyone can see everything you are presenting. You want the space to work in your favor while presenting. Making it as comfortable as you can for yourself will increase your verbal presentation success.

Lastly, as briefly discussed in Chapter One, find out if the presentation will be inside or outside and plan accordingly.

WHEN

The date and time for the presentation are critical in your planning efforts. First and foremost for the verbal aspect of the presentation is the amount of time you will be given to present. Confirm whether that allotment includes time for questions and answers at the end of the presentation.

Once you have the defined time, you can develop your script or outline for the presentation. Working alone or with your team, walk through the project and set up both the visual and verbal presentations to support and align with one another. Typically in the first year of study, your presentations will be done with boards, models, and samples. Think about how they can be used to support the verbal presentation and write the outline accordingly.

© iStockphoto.com/Claudiad

WHY

The entire point of a presentation is to sell your ideas to the audience. The verbal presentation is the key to that success. Make sure the presentation addresses any project requirements and your unique design solution.

Support the visual aids with design vocabulary, education, and information. You want the audience to buy into or select your project, and you want the intended clients to understand your design.

For you, as a student, you also want to get a good grade. Students ask me all the time how they can change their project to get a better grade. One of the easiest ways is to increase your verbal presentation skills. If you are confident and passionate about your design it makes it hard for the professor not to be.

© iStockphoto.com/dolgachov

© iStockphoto.com/shironosov

HOW

The "how" seems like it would be the easiest part of the verbal presentation: get up and talk about your project. But in reality, it is probably the hardest because most people are not confident speaking in front of others. Add to that the pressure that comes from presenting something you created and are invested in, and it's even more intimidating. Remember, a smile goes a long way.

© iStockphoto.com/skynesher

© iStockphoto.com/Yuri

To make the verbal presentation easier, all you need is a script that supports the visual aids. As stated previously and in other areas of this book, create both portions together for the greatest success and then practice.

Create note cards with key topics you want to discuss or, better yet, have the visual presentation force you to discuss issues through their layout and information. Use each and every item on your visual presentation. There is nothing worse than seeing a great drawing or model and not being told anything about it. Remember to sell your ideas through any means possible. If it is at your disposal, use it.

Finally, interact with your visual aids. Point to items on the boards—with clean, well-manicured fingernails. If you bite your nails, use a pointer or pen to do this. I remember attending my first presentation and all I could look at was the person's hangnails. I could not pay attention to what they were saying or pointing to because I was so distracted.

The "how" portion of the verbal presentation is probably the most important, so practice it, know your work and the facts about it, and sell your ideas to the audience.

EXERCISE

||||||||||||||||||||||||||||||||||||||||||||||||||||||||||||||||||||||||||||||||||||||||||||||||||||||||||||||||||||||||||||||

To increase your presentation skills and reinforce the topics discussed thus far, complete this two-part exercise.

Choose a general topic not related to design (food, football, etc.) for every person in your group. Quickly draw or find images and examples of the topic to pin up on the wall. After some time to prepare, each person should talk about their topic for five minutes.

- Begin each presentation with everyone watching the presenter.
- Designate a timekeeper.
    - Part one should continue for the entire five minutes.
    - Part two should begin two minutes into the presentation.

PART ONE:

- Have each person in the audience clap, or snap in larger groups, each time the presenter says their "um" word. Every person has a word or short phrase that they say when they speak, and it quickly will become obvious what each person's "um" word is.
    - Have one person keep a tally of each time the group claps, or snaps, for each person.

PART TWO:

- Everyone in the audience should put one arm up, resting their elbow on a table or their hand on their hip so as not to be too distracting.

- The presenter should take the time to make eye contact with each person in the room.

- After the presenter makes eye contact with an audience member, that person can lower their arm.

  - The presenter must continue their presentations, using their visual aids and watching their "ums," while also making eye contact with each member of the audience.

TIPS:

- This can quickly become embarrassing for the presenter, especially the first one, but everyone will eventually see that they all have their own "um" words, and everyone has a hard time making eye contact. The rest of the group will become supportive as they continue to see the presentations and finally have their turn.

- Once your word or phrase is identified, try to replace it by just stopping and taking a breath or pausing. This exercise is mainly about slowing down and being aware of what you are saying. An "um" word is usually space filler for when you are thinking.

EVALUATION:

General:

- Did they introduce themselves before they began?
- Did they end within the time limit?
- Did they ask for any comments or questions at the end of their presentation?
- Did they use the visual aids?

For Part One:

- Review the tally of how many times each person said their "um" word and identify who else uses that same word.
    - Pair up with another group member who uses the same or similar words, to assist each other when you present in the future.
        - Practice the presentation with that partner.
        - Before the actual presentation identify where your partner is sitting and look to them when you are getting flustered or for reassurance.
        - Have them keep tally of how many times you used the "um" word. After a few presentations that number will be greatly reduced.

For Part Two:

- Did they make eye contact with everyone or did they just go one by one down the row?
- Practice scanning the room to engage each person.

SUMMARY

IIIIIIIIIIIIIIIIIIIIIIIIIIIIIIIIIIIIIIIIIIIIIIIIIIIIIIIIIIIIIIIIIIIIIIIIIIIIIIIIIIIIIIIIIIIIIIIIIIIIIIIIIIIIIIIIIIIIIIIIIIIIIII

A successful presentation has two critical parts: the visual and the verbal presentation. Creating and practicing them together produces the best results, but the passion and confidence required for the verbal presentation can make all the difference. It can be the tipping factor in the final outcome for earning a good grade or getting a job.

FOUR

BUSINESS ETIQUETTE

OBJECTIVES

You will be able to understand and develop skills in etiquette when:

- Giving a design presentation
- Giving or attending a meeting
- Attending a networking event
- Leaving a phone message or writing an email
- Attending an event that includes dining

ETIQUETTE IS A LOST ART FOR SOME, WHILE OTHERS CONSIDER IT A LITTLE TOO STUFFY; BUT IN REALITY IT IS JUST GOOD BUSINESS SENSE TO USE GOOD MANNERS IN EVERY AREA OF YOUR LIFE. THIS CHAPTER IS AN ABBREVIATED APPROACH TO BASIC MANNERS IN TYPICAL SITUATIONS YOU WILL FIND YOURSELF IN WHILE ATTENDING SCHOOL AND THEN OUT IN THE INDUSTRY AFTER GRADUATION. WHEN I PROPOSED THIS SERIES OF BOOKS TO OUR ADVISORY BOARD, A GROUP OF INDUSTRY PROFESSIONALS FROM EVERY AREA IN THE DESIGN PROFESSION AND ACROSS THE COUNTRY, THEY THOUGHT THIS CHAPTER WAS A GREAT IDEA, BECAUSE THEY HAVE SEEN THE USE OF GOOD MANNERS DECREASE OVER THE PAST TWO DECADES.

PRESENTATIONS AND MEETINGS

For all intents and purposes, a presentation is a meeting. First, you want to do your homework about where the meeting is being held. If it is off-site, get directions and any parking suggestions from the venue where you are going to have the meeting. They may recommend a convenient place to park or a place where they will validate for the cost of parking. You may also want to ask if the parking is adjacent to the meeting location or if there is a place to park temporarily if you need to unload items for a large presentation or if a model or food order needs to be delivered by someone outside of your company, class, or business.

Second, you should ask about the room or area where the presentations are taking place so that you can plan accordingly, as discussed in Chapter One. Do not rely on the staff of the event site to have everything you need; make a contingency plan. Even something as simple as bringing thumbtacks to a critique space within your school can benefit not only you but your classmates as well.

If you are going to present electronically, bring an extra copy of the presentation and make sure that all of the fonts and images you have used are embedded in the file. The best way to do this is to save the file as a PDF. Lastly, bring a printout of your presentation. If all else fails you can make copies, if the facility provides for copying, and present as people follow along. Although this is not ideal, it will at least make the meeting worthwhile.

© iStockphoto.com/JOHNGOMEZPIX

© iStockphoto.com/BryanBrayley-Willmetts

Try to arrive no more than five minutes ahead of time. If you must leave a meeting or presentation early, let the organizer know in advance. The same is true if you will need to step out for a call during the presentation, although this should be avoided. Be courteous about the amount of time you are given during the presentation. The organizer needs to keep things running smoothly, which cannot happen if people run over their allotted time. Finally, turn off your cell phone and do not read emails or write or respond to texts during the presentation; even if the organizer is doing so, it is just unprofessional.

© iStockphoto.com/jaroon

On the day of the event, be prepared by having practiced what you are going to say and do for the presentation. As discussed throughout this book, the actual layout of your presentation can help with this task. If you know you want to discuss your overall concept first, then include that on your first board or slide. Use trigger words or images on your presentation to prompt you to comment about a particular item in your design. Make sure you discuss or reference everything that is in your presentation—if you do not, then why did you waste the time and presentation real estate to include the item?

Begin your presentation by introducing yourself to the panel, students, or other guests. Walk them through your presentation, and at the end ask for any questions or comments; do not just say, "That's it!" Conclude with a statement summarizing your presentation, and then thank the audience for their time and invite their input. In a formal setting, shaking the hands of the people you are presenting to may be appropriate. When in doubt, look to the senior-most person in the meeting and mirror his or her actions.

© iStockphoto.com/CEFutcher

TIPS:

- Do you have all of the items for your presentation—boards, drawings, models, samples, etc.—and enough copies of each?

- Do you know where you will be presenting, and does the venue have all the equipment and display items you need for a successful presentation?

- Do you know how you are going to begin and end your presentation within the time allotted, and have you rehearsed it to be sure?

- Do you have a friend or colleague who can take notes for you while you present? This can be helpful later on when you need to update or change your project.

INDUSTRY AND NETWORKING EVENTS

Like other meetings or presentations, industry events are a great way to meet new people and learn new things. Even as a student, and some would say *especially* as a student, you should attend these sorts of events to expand your network for when it is time to get an internship or job. Attending professional association and industry events also shows that you are serious about the profession you will be joining, and your participation also looks impressive on a résumé.

© iStockphoto.com/Andresr

While you are at these events, mingle with everyone—not just the people you came with; how else will you get to know other people? If you are shy, it is completely appropriate for you to ask a friend, colleague, or even the host to introduce you to people. When they do, act professional and smile, and give them your name and a good solid handshake while looking them in the eye. If appropriate after a discussion, ask for a business card, especially if they say to call or email them. This again shows them that you understand the business world and that you want to take advantage of that; but remember to follow up. Once you get better at small talk and know more people at these events, use the opportunity to assist others like you were assisted at these events. You will be a better colleague and more valuable to the profession when you help others and are seen as someone who is helpful.

© iStockphoto.com/StockRocket

TIPS:

- Be professional at all times and not standoffish. If you drink alcohol at these events do so in moderation.

- Perhaps go to the event with a person or company in mind that you would like to connect with and make that a goal for the evening.

- Use this opportunity to meet people higher up in the industry or at other companies and increase your industry network.

PHONE AND EMAIL

When leaving a voicemail make sure you state your name and the reason for your call, and then include your phone number—and say it twice, slowly—once at the beginning and once at the conclusion of the message. You can also leave the best time to reach you at that number or suggest that they email you back. If that is the case, leave your email address, twice, and spell it out.

Never leave more than one voicemail a day on the same topic and never leave the exact same message twice. Try to think about all the things you might want to discuss with the person and leave one compact and direct message. Do not call them several times a day with yet another thing you forgot to say. Make a list if you have to so you can stay on point.

© iStockphoto.com/nicolesy

Cellphone use is becoming an issue, and most people have written off bad etiquette as acceptable in the mainstream; but it is not. This portion of the chapter may make you roll your eyes, but it is an important area of etiquette that needs to be discussed as a reminder.

Remember to turn your phone off while in meetings, presentations, lectures, and studio times. If there is something very urgent that might happen, have the phone on vibrate and let the other people around you know that you could be interrupted.

Try to keep your conversations private. If you are in public, be aware that people can hear what you are saying, so try to keep a ten-foot zone around you and do not discuss delicate issues on your cellphone. Those types of issues should be dealt with privately and in person.

Do not use your cellphone in the restroom, in public or privately. It is just plain unprofessional and inconsiderate to those around you.

© iStockphoto.com/badmanproduction

© iStockphoto.com/alephx01

Emailing has become second nature to everyone, but etiquette should still be used when doing business with it, including emailing a professor or colleague. Watch your spelling and punctuation, and do not use all capital letters (that is considered shouting) or acronyms (they are either too casual or office/school-specific and not everyone will understand them) or emoticons (☺) in emails.

© iStockphoto.com/ChristopherBernard

Watch very carefully when using "reply all," versus just "reply." Another colleague of mine was fired after she sent an email to the entire company by hitting "reply all" instead of "forward" with an off-color message about the person who originally sent the message. Also, do not respond right away to an email that you perceive as negative. Take a moment and reread the email, write your response, but then save the draft of your response until you have had some time to take in the information and process what was really being said. Reread your reply later or, better yet, even the next day, before you send it. Similarly, think about what you are writing to someone else and consider how he or she could interpret it. Again, perhaps save the draft and read it later before sending it. Ultimately, it might be best to meet in person.

Always use an appropriate email address and signature. Get a Gmail or Yahoo account specifically for a job search with an address that is simply your name—not a nickname, catchphrase, or something inappropriate. Think about using this account for professional purposes only. This way you won't be sending spam to potential employers. Also, you can use this address forever, unlike your school or work addresses, which can change (and your résumé may be in someone's file for a while). You would hate to miss an opportunity simply because it went to the wrong email address. Create a standard signature for your emails with your name and contact information.

Finally, look at all the other electronic media and search for your name online. See what others can learn about you online without even trying very hard.

Consider using social and business networking sites such as LinkedIn, and check out the websites of firms, professional industry organizations, and magazines and blogs, too. It is much easier to contact a person at a firm when you can say that you saw their work in such-and-such magazine; and then say that you went to the firm's site and noticed that they do a lot of hospitality design. Then, you can mention seeing that they were the senior designer on such-and-such project, and according to LinkedIn, they also worked for ABC Firm as well. You could mention that you would really like to see if you could grab a cup of coffee or meet up at an industry event to chat.

All of those electronic connections could result in a face-to-face connection, and who knows where that could lead?

TIPS:

- Emails should be treated like letters and kept as formal as possible in specific settings such as business and school.

- When in doubt do not send an email or voicemail; try to meet with someone in person.

DINING

||||||||||||||||||||||||||||||||||||||||||||||||||||||||||||||||||||||||||||||||||||||||||||||||||||||||||||||||||||

You will find that some business meetings take place over lunch or dinner with a client or potential employer. The first challenge of dining etiquette usually comes in dealing with a place setting.

1A, 1B, 1C, AND 1D: DINNER PLATE, DINNER KNIFE, AND DINNER FORK

- 1a: The dinner plate may or may not be on the table when you arrive, and if it is, it may just be a placeholder for a soup or salad course that will come later.

- 1b and 1c: These are the dinner knife and fork. The knife is closest to the plate on the right and the fork on the left. When you are done eating, place your knife and fork diagonally across the plate with both handles pointing down and to the right, this will indicate to the server you are done with your meal. Never put them on the table.

- 1d: Teaspoon. The teaspoon is located to the right of the dinner knife.

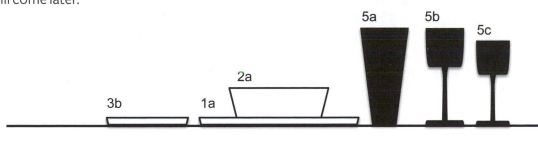

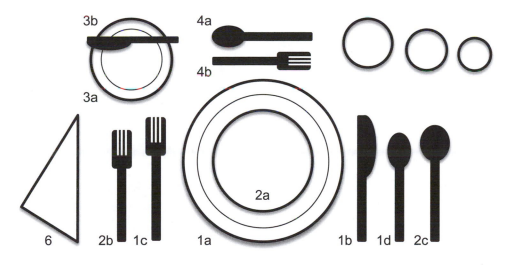

2A, 2B, AND 2C: SOUP OR SALAD BOWL AND TWO UTENSILS

- 2a: The soup or salad bowls may or may not be on the table when you arrive.

- 2b: The salad fork will be always be located on the outermost left side of the place setting. When you are using a salad fork, leave it in the bowl between bites so you don't get food on the table. The salad fork should be left in the bowl when you are done with your salad.

- 2c: The soup spoon will typically be the larger spoon on the table on the outside of the teaspoon. It may be brought to the table with the soup course instead. Just like the salad fork, it should be left in the bowl between bites and when you are done with the soup. Soup should be eaten by dipping the spoon into the center of the bowl and then moving the spoon away from you to avoid spills. Do not blow on the soup; wait for it to cool. Finally, it is proper to tip a soup bowl to get the last bites out, but never, ever, lift the bowl to your mouth to drink it.

3A AND 3B: BREAD PLATE AND BUTTER KNIFE

- 3a: The bread plate is found on the left side of the setting, just above the fork tines. Bread should be broken into bite-size pieces and not cut or buttered as one piece. You should place a pat or serving of butter on the edge of your bread plate and use it as needed.

- 3b: The butter knife is found horizontally across the bread plate. It is used to take the butter from the serving dish to the side of the plate and to butter each bite of bread. Put it back on the plate each time you are done using it and never put it on the table.

4A AND 4B: DESSERT SPOON AND CAKE FORK

- 4a: The dessert spoon is located above the plate, as is 4b, the cake fork. These may be brought to the table with the dessert course or be set at the table already.

5A, 5B, AND 5C: GLASSWARE

- 5a: The water glass tends to be the largest of the glasses and is located just above the top of the knife.

- 5b: The red wine glass is just to the right of the water glass and tends to be smaller than it.

- 5c: The white wine glass is the smallest of the glasses and should be held by the stem in order to keep the chill of the wine. This is not the case with red wine.

- Never turn a wine glass over to indicate that you do not want to drink wine. Wait for the server to come to the table and ask. Then you can decline and the glasses will be taken away.

6: NAPKIN

- When you sit down at the table, place the napkin in your lap. If the napkin is white and you are wearing black clothes, you may ask for a black one instead to avoid lint. In some restaurants, they will have them. You might want to take your cue from others at the table on this.

Napkins should go in your lap as soon as you sit down, following the host's lead. If you are interviewing or at a business dinner, wait for the most senior person to place the napkin in their lap and then follow suit. At some high-end restaurants the hostess will place your napkin in your lap.

If you need to get up from your seat at any time, loosely fold your napkin and place it near your plate. Do not put it on the seat or back of your chair. The reason for this is if there was food on the napkin, it could be transferred to the seat or chair back, causing a stain on your clothing or the chair. In some cases the waitstaff may formally fold your napkin for you for when you return.

Another thing to note: If you find something like a bone in your mouth, do not put it in the napkin. Instead, discreetly take it out of your mouth and put it on the side of your plate.

OTHER ETIQUETTE RULES

General family-style food etiquette says you pass from left to right. When food is served by waitstaff, it will be done from the left and cleared from the right. If someone asks for the salt and pepper, pass it to them first before you use it. Even if they ask for only the pepper, send them both, because as they get passed around someone else might want both.

There are some obvious rules that I am going to lay out as a gentle reminder. Do not season your food before tasting it. One executive takes senior people for a meal as their final interview, and he famously has not hired someone because they seasoned their food before they tasted it. He felt this was an indication of *assumption*, which is a trait he did not want in his leadership executives.

For hard-to-eat food such as corn, use your knife or a piece of bread to push the food onto your fork. Do not use your fingers. Obviously, do not talk with your mouth full or chew with your mouth open. And lastly, do not ask to try someone's food, and do not offer him or her a taste of yours.

Some other general rules are as follows: Use good posture at the table. Put your hands in your lap or rest your wrists on the edge of the table, but never put your forearms on the table. Try to pace yourself to finish your meal with the host or the majority of the group. Do not groom yourself at the table. Excuse yourself and go to the restroom.

TIPS:

- As a general rule, work your way in from the outside when using the utensils.

- When in doubt, watch the host or the most senior person in the room for clues about what to do and what utensil to use when. We have not discussed unusual utensils like an oyster fork or lobster utensil sets, so watch what others you are dining with do and follow along.

- When you first sit down at a formal table with large place settings, use the "B" and "D" trick under the table. On each hand, make a circle by touching the tips of your thumb and index finger together, then straighten out your other fingers. Your left hand will make a lowercase "B", and your right hand a lowercase "D." The B-side is your bread and the D-side is your drinks. If the person next to you starts to use your setting, you could teach them the trick; they will never make that mistake again.

EXERCISE

||||||||||||||||||||||||||||||||||||||||||||||||||||||||||||||||||||||||||||||||||||||||||

Break into three major groups in teams of two.

- **Group one:** Make a copy of the place setting seen on page 69 and identify each item and its use.

- **Group two:** Trade an email you sent to a peer or professor with your teammate and have them read and edit it for proper etiquette.

- **Group three:** Call each other's cell phone to evaluate the current greeting message, and then leave one with a suggestions of how it can be changed to be more professional.

EVALUATION:

- Did they get the place setting information correct? If not, did their partner help them out, or did they have to consult their books or notes?

- What changes did they make to the emails? Were they similar? Were they changes they would have to make to their own emails?

- What was the tone of the person's voice in the greeting message? Could you tell if the person was smiling (because you can)?

- What was the tone of the person's voice in the message? Were their comments constructive and helpful? Will they change their greeting message as a result?

SUMMARY

||||||||||||||||||||||||||||||||||||||||||||||||||||||||||||||||||||||||||||||||||||||||||

Etiquette in every form is an important part of business and your education. Simple steps and reminders can help keep you looking and sounding like a professional. Take opportunities to get yourself out there and engaged with your peers and the professional industry network while using proper etiquette. Starting now as a student will only make it easier when you go out into the profession.

FIVE

BODY LANGUAGE

OBJECTIVES

You will be able to identify and successfully understand:

- The implications of what your body language is saying to others
- The intentions behind the body language others demonstrate toward you

THE WORDS AND VISUAL AIDS YOU USE TO CONVEY YOUR DESIGN INTENTIONS ARE ONLY A SMALL PART OF WHAT YOU COMMUNICATE TO OTHERS WHEN GIVING A PRESENTATION OR ATTENDING A MEETING. IT VARIES SOME, BUT STATISTICALLY, IT IS SAID THAT YOUR BODY LANGUAGE——THAT IS, THE WAY YOU CARRY YOURSELF AND THE GESTURES YOU USE——MAKES UP MORE THAN HALF OF THE MESSAGE YOU ARE CONVEYING. ROUGHLY 10 PERCENT IS THE ACTUAL WORDS YOU ARE SPEAKING, WHILE THE OTHER 40 PERCENT IS TYPICALLY THE TONE OF YOUR VOICE. SOME PEOPLE EVEN BELIEVE THAT 90 PERCENT OF COMMUNICATION IS NONVERBAL.

You can use this information to your advantage, by understanding the generally accepted meanings behind some of the most common gestures and body language basics.

Caution should be taken when working with people from other cultures, as the meanings behind certain gestures could vary.

READING FACES

First, remember the importance of eye contact. Look at someone in the eyes and try to maintain periodic eye contact with each person at the presentation. This tells them you are interested and engaged with the conversation. Ideally, you will get a nod indicating they are interested and engaged as well.

A person typically blinks six to eight times a minute; however, when someone is stressed out, they will blink more often. If they close, rub, or cover their eyes, they are trying to block out the visual and verbal information they are receiving because it might be threatening or unwelcome.

© iStockphoto.com/mediaphotos

When someone lowers their gaze, like a child, it means they want your approval; however, when they peer over or take off their glasses, they are thinking and reflecting on what is being said and, therefore, are engaged in the presentation.

Raising their eyebrows is also a good sign, as they are curious and interested in what is being presented. Conversely, if they lower their eyebrows, it could mean they are confused or even fearful.

© iStockphoto.com/MarkHunt

© iStockphoto.com/LifesizeImages

Finally, when interacting with someone, watch where they are looking. If they are looking up and to the left, they are more than likely thinking and remembering something. On the other hand, looking up and to the right indicates that they are imagining and creating something. Both might be a good response, depending on the situation.

© iStockphoto.com/digitalskillet

GESTURES

As stated earlier, if someone nods with you, they are listening and possibly in agreement with you, a good sign when giving a presentation. Tilting your head means you are open to and evaluating the information, ready to cooperate with the individual or group. You can also be reflecting on the information.

© iStockphoto.com/aabejon

Stroking your chin or touching the bridge of your nose is a sign that also indicates that you are evaluating and reflecting on the information being presented. This is another good sign if you are looking for a reaction of understanding. However, scratching your nose means you may be lying.

Massaging your forehead or earlobes is a soothing gesture that can indicate you are uneasy or vulnerable.

Finally, proceed with caution if someone is chewing on a pencil or their lip, because it means they are nervous or under pressure.

© iStockphoto.com/energyy

READING BODIES

Standing straight with your feet shoulder-width apart and your weight evenly balanced makes you look relaxed yet confident. It signifies confidence and determination.

Slouching or standing with your weight unevenly distributed can make you look like you are not interested or enthusiastic about a topic. Leaning or moving toward people indicates you like them and are open and cooperative, while pulling away says your do not care for them and are not interested in what they are saying. If you are mirroring each other and positioned facing one another, it means you are building trust.

© iStockphoto.com/RichVintage

Shifting your weight either from side to side or front to back provides a comforting movement, but it also indicates you could be nervous, upset, or anxious.

Your body position in the room can also have an impact on what you are conveying. Turning your body and feet toward a person shows you are directing the information to them and is also a sign of respect. Be careful to pay attention to everyone in the room in a similar manner by giving them eye contact. When responding to questions, face the person who is speaking in order to hear what they are asking, and begin your response in that position. Engage others while answering and try to end facing the person who originally asked the question in order to get confirmation that you answered it properly.

Also, if someone approaches while you are already having a separate conversation and you want that person to feel invited to join in, turn the angle of your body outward to them, indicating they are welcome to the conversation.

© iStockphoto.com/Geber86

ARMS

Crossing your arms in front of your body could indicate anger, but when combined with crossed legs it means that you are confrontational or defensive. Be careful about this when meeting people for the first time—while it is a widely known body language indicator, for some people this is their natural stance.

A person with their arms held casually behind their back can be in an open and cooperative mood, while at other times and combined with other indicators, it can mean they are frustrated.

© iStockphoto.com/4774344sean

© iStockphoto.com/macky_ch

GESTURES

Having an open stance and open hands means you are open and cooperative. Closed or fist-like gestures indicate you have a strong position and may not be open to change. It also means you could be defensive and confrontational.

© iStockphoto.com/Yuri_Arcurs

Fidgeting can indicate insecurity and nervousness, while gesturing in general means you are energetic and warm, interactive and engaging. Those who gesture less are logical and rational.

Conversely, hiding your hands in your pockets or under the table can mean you have something to hide or are insecure or nervous. Rubbing your thumbs over and over each other is another indication of nervousness.

© iStockphoto.com/4x6

Biting your nails or touching your cuticles is a sign of low confidence and nervousness, while steepling—creating a tower-like gesture by placing your elbows on the table and fingertips together—doesn't allow you to bite your nails and also helps you seem more self-confident.

When sitting at a table, spread out as much as you can. The more space you take up, the more important you are perceived to be.

If a person gets up from the table to point to something being presented, or interacts with a portion of the presentation, it is always a good sign. The person is fully engaged and interested in the project.

© iStockphoto.com/Photomorphic

SUMMARY

Some body language can be reactionary, but it is typically genuine. Remember, every individual has his or her own quirks, so the body language interpretations discussed in this chapter could vary, but are generally good rules of thumb to follow. In addition, several of them can be used in combination and change the definition drastically. As an example, a person standing with their arms crossed in front and swaying front to back with their hands in their pockets, can be seen as very confident with a large presence. Each of those signals individually would not have the same effect.

APPENDIX A: PRESENTATION CHECKLIST

LIST:

Drawings (check those needed and indicate the quantity or notes):

- Plans:

    _____ Site plan(s)

    _____ Floor plan(s)

    _____ Furniture plan(s)

    _____ Finish plan(s)

    _____ Engineering plan(s)—Mechanical, Plumbing, Electrical, Communication, etc.

    _____ Enlarged plan(s)

General Notes:
- Are notes necessary?
- What might be cross-referenced?
- Will the drawing be black-and-white or rendered?

- Elevations:

    ____ Exterior Elevation(s) for _____ side (north/south/east/west)

    ____ Exterior Elevation(s) for _____ side

    ____ Exterior Elevation(s) for _____ side

    ____ Exterior Elevation(s) for _____ side

    ____ Interior Elevation(s) for room _____

    ____ Interior Elevation(s) for room _____

    ____ Interior Elevation(s) for room _____

    ____ Interior Elevation(s) for room _____

General Notes:

- Are notes necessary?
- What might be cross-referenced?
- Will the drawing be black-and-white or rendered?

- Sections

    _____ Building Section through _____

    _____ Building Section through _____

    _____ Building Section through _____

    _____ Building Section through _____

    _____ Detail Section through _____

    _____ Detail Section through _____

    _____ Detail Section through _____

    _____ Detail Section through _____

General Notes:

- Are notes necessary?
- What might be cross-referenced?
- Will the drawing be black-and-white or rendered?

- Three-Dimensional Drawings

    _____ Axonometric of _____

    _____ Axonometric of _____

    _____ Axonometric of _____

    _____ Axonometric of _____

    _____ One-Point Perspective of _____

    _____ One-Point Perspective of _____

    _____ One-Point Perspective of _____

    _____ One-Point Perspective of _____

    _____ Two-Point Perspective of _____

    _____ Two-Point Perspective of _____

    _____ Two-Point Perspective of _____

    _____ Two-Point Perspective of _____

General Notes:

- Are notes necessary?
- What might be cross-referenced?
- Will the drawing be black-and-white or rendered?

- Other Items

  _____ Concept Statement

  _____ Client Description

  _____ Diagrams* with text or without text

  _____ Diagrams* with text or without text

  _____ Diagrams* with text or without text

  _____ Diagrams* with text or without text

  _____ Materials and Finishes: Size per material?

      _____ Legend

      _____ Key

  _____ Furniture: Size per furniture photograph?

      _____ Legend

      _____ Key

  _____ Models

*Diagrams are simple graphic drawings that enhance the presentation by showing the design intent or clarifying other issues.

MOUNTAIN CABIN

Design Concept:

xxxxxxxxxxxxxxxxxxxxxxxxxxxxxxxxxxxxxxx
xxxxxxxxxxxxxxxxxxxxxxxxxxxxxxxxxxxxxxx
xxxxxxxxxxxxxxxxxxxxxxxxxxxxxxxxxxxxxxx
xxxxxxxxxxxxxxxxxxxxxxxxxxxxxxxxxxxxxxx
xxxxxxxxxxxxxxxxxxxxxxxxxxxxxxxxxxxxxxx
xxxxxxxxxxxxxxx

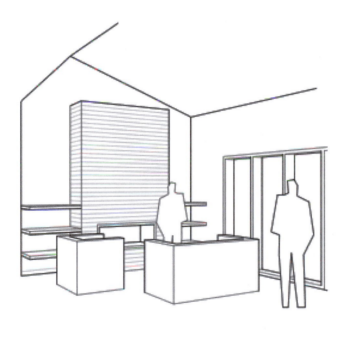

Fireplace Perspective

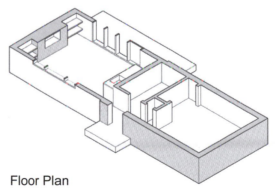

Floor Plan

MOUNTAIN CABIN

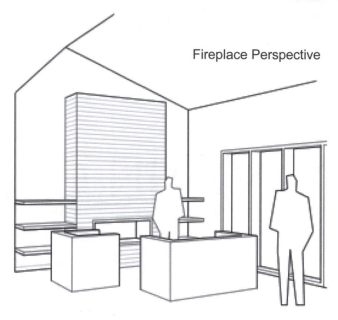

Fireplace Perspective

Design Concept:

xxxxxxxxxxxxxxxxxxxxxxxxxxxxxxxxxxxxxxxxxxxxxxxxxxxxx
xxxxxxxxxxxxxxxxxxxxxxxxxxxxxxxxxxxxxxxxxxxxxxxxxxxxx
xxxxxxxxxxxx

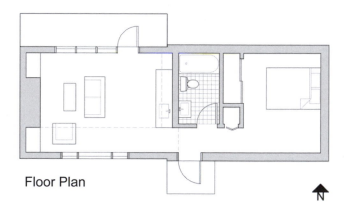

Floor Plan

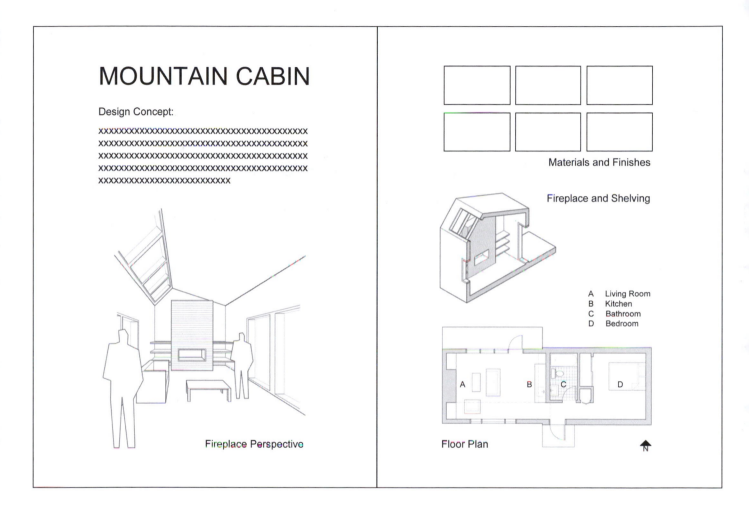

MOUNTAIN CABIN

Design Concept:

xxxxxxxxxxxxxxxxxxxxxxxxxxxxxxxxxxxxxxxxxxxx
xxxxxxxxxxxxxxxxxxxxxxxxxxxxxxxxxxxxxxxxxxxx
xxxxxxxxxxxxxxxxxxxxxxxxxxxxxxxxxxxxxxxxxxxx
xxxxxxxxxxxxxxxxxxxxxxxxxxxxxxxxxxxxxxxxxxxx
xxxxxxxxxxxxxxxxxxxxxxxxxxxx

Fireplace Perspective

Materials and Finishes

Fireplace and Shelving

A   Living Room
B   Kitchen
C   Bathroom
D   Bedroom

Floor Plan

MOUNTAIN

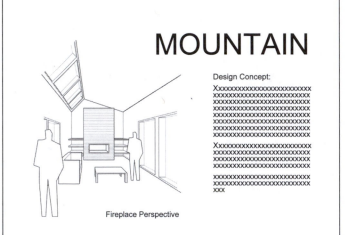

Design Concept:

Xxxxxxxxxxxxxxxxxxxxxxxxx
xxxxxxxxxxxxxxxxxxxxxxxxx
xxxxxxxxxxxxxxxxxxxxxxxxx
xxxxxxxxxxxxxxxxxxxxxxxxx
xxxxxxxxxxxxxxxxxxxxxxxxx
xxxxxxxxxxxxxxxxxxxxxxxxx

Xxxxxxxxxxxxxxxxxxxxxxxxx
xxxxxxxxxxxxxxxxxxxxxxxxx
xxxxxxxxxxxxxxxxxxxxxxxxx
xxxxxxxxxxxxxxxxxxxxxxxxx
xxxxxxxxxxxxxxxxxxxxxxxxx
xxx

Fireplace Perspective

CABIN

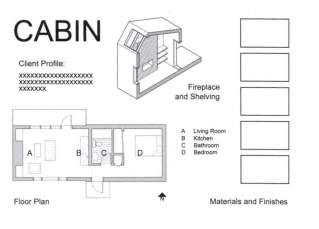

Client Profile:

xxxxxxxxxxxxxxxxxxx
xxxxxxxxxxxxxxxxxxx
xxxxxxx

Fireplace
and Shelving

A Living Room
B Kitchen
C Bathroom
D Bedroom

Floor Plan

Materials and Finishes

INDEX

Alignment, 37

Arms, 87

Arrows, north, 23

Audience

    presentation, 4–6

    size, 6

    verbal presentation, 46

AutoCAD, 10

Axonometric drawings, 21, 94

Board samples, mountain cabin, 97–100

Body language, 90

    arms, 87

    communication, 79

    gestures, 80, 83–84, 88–89

    reading bodies, 85–89

    reading faces, 81–84

Border, 40

Boundary, presentation, 36

Bread plate, etiquette, 70

Business etiquette. See etiquette

Business networking, 68

Butter knife, etiquette, 70

Cabin

    board samples, 97–100

    drawings, 17

    elevation example, 19

    oblique and axonometric drawing

        example, 21

    one- and two-point perspective

        examples, 22

    plan examples, 18

    project titles, 27

    section example, 20

Cake fork, etiquette, 71

Calendar, presentation, 9–10

Cartoon presentations, 35–36

Cell phone, etiquette, 59, 66, 75

Checklist, presentation, 91–95

Communication. See body language

    cell phone, 59, 66, 75

    email, 65, 67–68

Contingency plan, 58

Crowding, 39

Date and time, presentation, 9–10, 48

Design vocabulary, 4, 49

Dessert spoon, etiquette, 71

Diagrams, 95

Dining etiquette

    bread plate and butter knife, 70

    dessert spoon and cake fork, 71

    dinner plate, knife and fork, 69

    glassware, 71

    napkin, 72

    place setting, 69

    soup or salad bowl and utensils, 70

Drawing selection

    communicating design, 17

    elevations, 19

    oblique and axonometric drawings, 21

    one- and two-point perspectives, 22

    plans, 18

    sections, 20

Electronic media, 68

Electronic presentations, 35, 58

Elevations, 19, 92

    section-cut symbol, 26

    symbols, 25

Email, etiquette, 65, 67–68

    exercise activity, 75

Etiquette, 57

    dining, 69–73

    evaluation, 76

    exercise activity, 75–76

    family-style dining, 73

    general rules, 73

    industry events, 63–64

    networking events, 63–64

    phone and email, 65–68

    presentations and meetings, 58–62

    tips, 74

Exercise

    etiquette, 75–76

    presentation skills, 52–54

Eye contact, 53, 81–83

Faces, reading, 81–84

File storage, 10

Fireplace

    perspective of, in cabin, 97–100

    section of, 17

    wall elevation, 19

Floor plan, 17, 18

    cabin, 97–100

    drawing titles, 28

    labels, 30

    legends and keys, 31–32

    section-cut symbol, 26

Formatting, 37

Gestures, 80

    cultures, 80

    facial, 83–84

    reading bodies, 88–89

Glassware, etiquette, 71

Gmail, 68

Graphic symbols

    elevation, 25

    floor plan, 32

    north arrows, 23

    plan, 18

Graphic symbols (*continued*)
    scales, 24
    section-cut, 26
Grids, 38–39

Industry events, etiquette, 63–64
Introductions, presentation, 61

Keys, drawings, 31–32, 95
Kitchen wall, elevation, 19

Labels, 30
Layouts, presentation, 33, 39, 40
Legends, drawings, 31–32, 40, 95
LinkedIn, 68
Location, presentation, 8, 47, 58

Materials and finishes, 95, 99, 100
Meetings, etiquette, 58–62
Mock presentations, 35–36

Napkin, etiquette, 72
Need, presentation, 34
Networking events, etiquette, 63–64
North arrows, symbols, 23
North elevation, 17
Note cards, 51

Oblique drawings, 21
One-by-one grid, 38
One-point perspectives, 22, 94

Parking, 58
Perspectives
    drawing, 17
    one- and two-point, 22, 94
Phone, etiquette, 65–68
"Pin-up" critique presentation, 11
Place setting, etiquette, 69
    exercise activity, 75
Plans, 91. *See also* floor plan
    drawing selection, 18
    section-cut symbol, 26

Posture
    etiquette, 73
    reading bodies, 85–86
PowerPoint, 35
Practice, 51, 54, 59, 62
Presentation. *See also* verbal presentation
    alignment, 37
    audience, 4–6, 46
    board samples, 97–100
    calendar, 9–10, 48
    cartoon, 35–36
    checklist, 91–95
    content, 7, 47
    creation of, 7
    determining need, 34
    etiquette, 58–62
    exercising skills, 52–54
    formatting, 37
    general text, 29
    grids, 38–39
    how, 12
    labels, 30
    layouts, 33, 39, 40
    location, 8, 47
    mock, 35–36
    process, 50–51
    projects with multiple sheets, 40
    project titles, 27
    purpose, 11, 49
Presentation drawings, 16
    drawing titles, 28
    elevations, 19
    oblique and axonometric drawings, 21
    one- and two-point
        perspectives, 22
    plans, 18
    sections, 20
    selection, 17
Presentation format, 6
Prezi, 35
Professional, 63, 64, 77
Project titles, 27
Public exhibit, 11

Revit, 10
Roof plan, 17. *See also* floor plan; plans

Salad bowl and fork, etiquette, 70
Scales, drawings, 24, 36
Script, 51
Section, 93
    drawings, 20
    fireplace, 17
Section-cut symbols, 26
Smile, 50, 63, 64
Social networking, 68
Software, 10, 35
Soup bowl and spoon, etiquette, 70
Spacing, 37, 39
Symbols. *See* graphic symbols

Technical drawings, 16
Text, 29
Three-dimensional drawings, 22, 94
Time, etiquette, 59
Time and date, presentation, 9–10, 48
Time management, 9
Titles. 27, 28
Two-point perspectives, 22, 94

"Um" words, 52, 53

Verbal presentation. *See also* presentation
    audience, 46
    date and time, 48
    preparation, 45–51
    purpose, 49
Visual aids
    design vocabulary, 49
    preparation, 47
Vocabulary, audience, 4, 49
Voicemail, etiquette, 65, 76

"Why" aspect, presentation, 11

Yahoo account, 68